Recipes of The Roaring Twenties

A Vintage Cookbook Taking You Back in Time to the 1920s

Copyright Material

© 2023 Steven Masters

All Rights Reserved

No part of this book may be used or transmitted in any form or by any means without the proper written consent of the publisher and copyright owner, except for brief quotations used in a review. This book should not be considered a substitute for medical, legal, or other professional advice.

Sign-up Now
and Be Notified of New Books

Website: readbooks.today

Table of Contents

INTRODUCTION ... 1

COCKTAILS ... 4

CLASSIC MARTINI ... 5
SIDECAR ... 6
BEE'S KNEES ... 7
FRENCH 75 ... 8
CLOVER CLUB ... 9
MARY PICKFORD ... 10
BOULEVARDIER ... 11
GIN RICKEY ... 12
MINT JULEP ... 13
OLD FASHIONED ... 14

APPETIZERS ... 15

DEVILED EGGS ... 16
OYSTERS ROCKEFELLER ... 17
SHRIMP COCKTAIL ... 18
WALDORF SALAD ... 19
CELERY VICTOR ... 20
STUFFED MUSHROOMS ... 21
CLAMS CASINO ... 22
LOBSTER NEWBURG ... 23
ASPARAGUS VINAIGRETTE ... 24
TOMATO ASPIC ... 25

ENTREES ... 26

CHICKEN A LA KING ... 27
BEEF WELLINGTON ... 28
LOBSTER THERMIDOR ... 30
SOLE VERONIQUE ... 31
CHICKEN TETRAZZINI ... 32
OYSTERS BIENVILLE ... 34
DUCK A L'ORANGE ... 36
EGGS BENEDICT ... 38
VEAL OSCAR ... 40
STEAK DIANE ... 41
COQ AU VIN ... 42

Salmon Mousse	44
Tournedos Rossini	45
Pork Tenderloin with Apples	46
Grilled Lamb Chops with Mint Jelly	47
Filet Mignon with Béarnaise Sauce	48
Corned Beef and Cabbage	49
Lobster à l'Américaine	50
Pot-au-Feu	52
Chicken Marengo	54
Seafood Newburg	56
Veal Piccata	57
Stuffed Bell Peppers	58
Chicken Cordon Bleu	59
Chateaubriand	60

DESSERTS — 61

Pineapple Upside-Down Cake	62
Baked Alaska	64
Chocolate Soufflé	65
Charlotte Russe	66
Fruit Cocktail with Chantilly Cream	67
Opera Cake	68
Strawberry Shortcake	70
Raspberry Meringue	72
Jellied Fruit Terrine	73

Introduction

The Roaring Twenties, a decade that spanned from 1920 to 1929, was a time of significant cultural, social, and political change. It was an era characterized by rapid economic growth, urbanization, and technological advancements that transformed how people lived, worked, and entertained themselves. The term "roaring" describes the exuberant, freewheeling popular culture that emerged during this period. The United States, in particular, saw an outpouring of creativity, artistic expression, and innovative ideas that would leave a lasting impact on the world.

The end of World War I in 1918 and the subsequent peace brought a renewed sense of optimism and prosperity. People were eager to leave behind the hardships and traumas of the war years and embrace a new era of progress and hope. The economy boomed, and the introduction of consumer credit made luxury goods and services accessible to a broader range of people. The automobile industry flourished, and mass production techniques like the assembly line led to the increased affordability of cars, which in turn revolutionized transportation and spurred the growth of suburbs.

In the cultural sphere, the Roaring Twenties was an era marked by the rise of jazz, a uniquely American musical genre that originated in African American communities. Jazz quickly became popular across the country, and its upbeat rhythms and improvisational style perfectly embodied the spirit of the time. In addition, the Harlem Renaissance, a cultural movement among African American artists, writers, and intellectuals, also flourished during this decade, celebrating Black culture and asserting the importance of racial equality and self-expression.

Fashion also underwent a significant transformation in the 1920s, with women casting off the restrictive garments of the previous era in favor of looser, more comfortable clothing. The flapper, an icon of the Roaring Twenties, emerged as a symbol of the modern, independent woman. Flappers were known for their short, bobbed hairstyles, dropped-waist dresses, and energetic dancing. The adoption of trousers by women and the popularity of sportswear also signified a shift towards more practical and comfortable clothing.

The rise of the motion picture industry also marked the 1920s. Hollywood became the epicenter of film production, and the advent of "talkies," or films with synchronized sound, revolutionized the medium. Silent film stars like Charlie Chaplin and Mary Pickford gave way to new celebrities like Greta Garbo and Clara Bow, who captivated audiences with their glamour and talent. Going to the cinema became a popular pastime, and the influence of Hollywood on fashion, culture, and society was immense.

However, the Roaring Twenties was not without its darker side. Prohibition, the nationwide ban on the production, sale, and transportation of alcohol in the United States, led to the rise of organized crime and illegal speakeasies where people could drink and socialize in secret. Social tensions, including racial strife, labor disputes, and the rise of nativism and xenophobia, also marked the decade. Despite these challenges, the Roaring Twenties remains an iconic historical period known for its glamour, cultural achievements, and optimism permeating the era. The distinctive style of the time, with its Art Deco architecture, jazz music, and elegant fashions, continues to inspire and captivate people today. In addition, the Roaring Twenties was a time of great innovation and change, leaving an indelible mark on the world and shaping the course of the 20th century.

The Roaring Twenties was a time of opulence and indulgence in the culinary world. The newfound prosperity and the desire to celebrate life to the fullest after the hardships of the war years led to an explosion of creativity in the kitchen. Dishes like Lobster Newburg, Beef Wellington, and Baked Alaska were popular, reflecting the extravagant tastes and elegance of the era. The rise of cocktail culture was also a significant development during the 1920s, with speakeasies and sophisticated gatherings serving a variety of classic concoctions that are still beloved today, such as the Martini, the Sidecar, and the Old Fashioned.

The style of dining during the Roaring Twenties was a reflection of the time's vibrant social scene. Dinner parties were an opportunity for hosts and hostesses to display their wealth and sophistication, with lavish table settings, formal attire, and a focus on presentation. Elaborate multi-course meals were often served, and guests would linger over their food and conversation for hours, accompanied by live music or entertainment.

The influence of the Roaring Twenties extended beyond the United States, with Europe and other parts of the world also experiencing cultural shifts and the embrace of modernity. In Paris, the epicenter of European art and culture, the period was known as Les Années Folles or the "Crazy Years." This era saw the emergence of innovative artistic movements like Surrealism and Art Deco, which would have a lasting impact on the aesthetics of the time and continue to influence design and art today.

One of the significant culinary trends of the 1920s was the growing popularity of international flavors and ingredients, as people became more adventurous in their tastes and eager to explore new culinary horizons. French cuisine, in particular, was highly regarded, and many classic French dishes became popular in American households and fine dining establishments. This fusion of cultures and flavors helped shape the Roaring Twenties' unique culinary landscape, offering a rich tapestry of tastes and experiences for diners to enjoy.

As the decade drew to a close, the Wall Street Crash of 1929 and the subsequent Great Depression brought an end to the prosperity and exuberance of the Roaring Twenties. The hardships that followed forced many people to reassess their priorities and adapt to a new reality. However, the legacy of the Roaring Twenties continues to resonate in our modern world. The innovations, cultural achievements, and unique style of the era have left an indelible mark on history, and the dishes and cocktails that were popular during the time continue to be enjoyed and celebrated today. By exploring and recreating the flavors of the Roaring Twenties, we can pay homage to this extraordinary period and keep the spirit of the era alive for future generations to enjoy.

Cocktails

Classic Martini

Prep: 2 minutes – Cook: 5 minutes – Servings: 1
Calories: 140 – Fat 0g – Carbs: 2g – Fiber: 0g – Sugar: 0g – Protein 0g

The classic martini is a simple and elegant cocktail that has been enjoyed for over a century. It's made with either gin or vodka, dry vermouth, and garnished with either a lemon twist or an olive.

Ingredients

- 2 ½ ounces gin or vodka
- Lemon twist or olive for garnish
- ½ ounce dry vermouth
- Ice

Directions

1. Chill a martini glass in the freezer for at least 10 minutes.
2. In a mixing glass or shaker, combine the gin or vodka and dry vermouth.
3. Fill the glass with ice and stir the mixture until it's very cold, about 30 seconds.
4. Strain the cocktail into the chilled martini glass. Garnish with a lemon twist or olive.

Sidecar

Prep: 2 minutes – Cook: 5 minutes – Servings: 1
Calories: 240 – Fat 0g – Carbs: 16g – Fiber: 0g – Sugar: 1g – Protein 0g

The Sidecar is a classic cocktail made with cognac or brandy, Cointreau, and lemon juice. It's a deliciously balanced drink that has been enjoyed for nearly a century

Ingredients

- 2 ounces cognac or brandy
- ¾ ounce fresh lemon juice
- Lemon twist for garnish
- 1 ounce Cointreau
- Sugar for rimming (optional)

Directions

1. If desired, rim a chilled cocktail glass with sugar by rubbing a slice of lemon around the rim and dipping it in sugar.
2. In a shaker filled with ice, combine the cognac or brandy, Cointreau, and lemon juice.
3. Shake vigorously until well chilled.
4. Strain the cocktail into the prepared glass. Garnish with a lemon twist and serve.

Bee's Knees

Prep: 2 minutes – Cook: 5 minutes – Servings: 1
Calories: 140 – Fat 0g – Carbs: 4g – Fiber: 0g – Sugar: 1g – Protein 0g

"Bee's knees" is an English idiom that originated in the 1920s and was popularized during the era of the flappers and the Jazz Age. The phrase is used to describe something or someone that is excellent, outstanding, or top-notch.

Ingredients

- ¾ ounce honey syrup (made by combining equal parts honey and hot water and stirring until honey is completely dissolved)
- 2-ounce gin
- ¾ ounce fresh lemon juice
- Ice
- Lemon twist or wheel, for garnish

Directions

1. In a cocktail shaker filled with ice, combine the gin, lemon juice, and honey syrup.
2. Shake vigorously until the outside of the shaker is frosty and cold.
3. Strain into a chilled cocktail glass.
4. Garnish with a lemon twist or wheel.

French 75

Prep: 2 minutes – Cook: 5 minutes – Servings: 1
Calories: 240 – Fat 0g – Carbs: 4g – Fiber: 0g – Sugar: 2g – Protein 0g

The French 75 is a classic cocktail that is typically made with gin, lemon juice, simple syrup, and sparkling wine. It is named after the French 75mm field gun, a powerful piece of artillery used during World War I and is said to have been created in the early 20th century at Harry's New York Bar in Paris.

Ingredients

- 2 ounces gin
- ½ ounce simple syrup
- 1-ounce fresh lemon juice
- 2 ounces chilled sparkling wine
- Ice
- Lemon twist or wheel, for garnish

Directions

1. In a cocktail shaker filled with ice, combine the gin, lemon juice, and simple syrup.
2. Shake vigorously until the outside of the shaker is frosty and cold.
3. Strain into a chilled champagne flute or coupe glass.
4. Top with the chilled sparkling wine. Garnish with a lemon twist or wheel.

Clover Club

Prep: 2 minutes – Cook: 5 minutes – Servings: 1
Calories: 220 – Fat 2g – Carbs: 6g – Fiber: 1g – Sugar: 1g – Protein 1g

The Clover Club is a classic cocktail that has been around since the late 19th century. It is a gin-based cocktail that also includes lemon juice, raspberry syrup, and egg white, which gives it a frothy texture and a smooth, silky finish.

Ingredients

- ¾ ounce fresh lemon juice
- 2 ounces gin
- 1 egg white
- Ice
- ¾ ounce raspberry syrup
- Fresh raspberries, for garnish (optional)

Directions

1. In a cocktail shaker, combine the gin, lemon juice, raspberry syrup, and egg white.
2. Shake vigorously without ice for about 10 seconds to emulsify the egg white.
3. Add ice to the shaker and shake again for about 10 seconds to chill and dilute the cocktail.
4. Strain the mixture into a chilled coupe glass. Garnish with fresh raspberries, if desired.

Mary Pickford

Prep: 2 minutes – Cook: 5 minutes – Servings: 1
Calories: 120 – Fat 0g – Carbs: 2g – Fiber: 1g – Sugar: 2g – Protein 0g

The Mary Pickford is a classic cocktail named after the famous silent film actress Mary Pickford. It is a rum-based cocktail that also includes pineapple juice, grenadine, and maraschino liqueur, which gives it a fruity and slightly sweet taste.

Ingredients

- ¼ ounce maraschino liqueur
- 2 ounces white rum
- ¼ ounce grenadine
- 2 ounces unsweetened pineapple juice
- Ice
- Pineapple wedge and/or maraschino cherry for garnish (optional)

Directions

1. In a cocktail shaker, combine the white rum, unsweetened pineapple juice, grenadine, and maraschino liqueur.
2. Add ice to the shaker and shake vigorously for about 10 seconds to chill and dilute the cocktail.
3. Strain the mixture into a chilled glass, such as a martini or coupe glass.
4. Garnish with a pineapple wedge and/or maraschino cherry, if desired.

Boulevardier

Prep: 2 minutes – Cook: 5 minutes – Servings: 1
Calories: 120 – Fat 0g – Carbs: 2g – Fiber: 0g – Sugar: 2g – Protein 0g

The Boulevardier is a classic cocktail that is similar to a Negroni but made with whiskey instead of gin. It is a perfect drink for whiskey lovers who enjoy the bitter and slightly sweet taste of a Negroni. The cocktail is typically made with equal parts of bourbon or rye whiskey, Campari, and sweet vermouth.

Ingredients

- 1 ounce Campari
- 1 ½ ounces rye whiskey or bourbon
- 1-ounce sweet vermouth
- Orange peel, for garnish

Directions

1. In a mixing glass or cocktail shaker, combine the bourbon or rye whiskey, Campari, and sweet vermouth.
2. Add ice to the shaker and stir for about 30 seconds to chill and dilute the cocktail.
3. Strain the mixture into a chilled glass, such as a rocks glass or coupe glass.
4. Garnish with an orange peel, expressing the oils over the drink before dropping it into the glass.

Gin Rickey

Prep: 2 minutes – Cook: 5 minutes – Servings: 1
Calories: 140 – Fat 0g – Carbs: 2g – Fiber: 0g – Sugar: 3g – Protein 0g

The Gin Rickey is a classic cocktail that is both refreshing and simple to make. It is a variation of the classic Rickey cocktail, which is typically made with bourbon or gin, lime juice, and soda water. The Gin Rickey is made with gin, lime juice, and soda water, and can be garnished with a lime wedge.

Ingredients

- 2 ounces gin
- 1-ounce fresh lime juice
- Club soda or soda water
- Lime wedge, for garnish

Directions

1. Fill a Collins glass or highball glass with ice.
2. Add the gin and lime juice to the glass and stir briefly.
3. Top up the glass with club soda or soda water.
4. Garnish with a lime wedge and serve.

Mint Julep

Prep: 2 minutes – Cook: 5 minutes – Servings: 1
Calories: 210 – Fat 0g – Carbs: 2g – Fiber: 0g – Sugar: 3g – Protein 0g

The Mint Julep is a classic cocktail that originated in the southern United States and is traditionally made with bourbon, fresh mint, sugar, and water. It is a refreshing and easy-to-make cocktail that is perfect for warm weather or as a refreshing summer drink.

Ingredients

- 2 ounces bourbon
- 1-ounce simple syrup (or 1 tsp granulated sugar)
- 8-10 fresh mint leaves
- Crushed ice
- Mint sprig, for garnish

Directions

1. In a Julep cup or rocks glass, muddle the mint leaves and simple syrup (or sugar) together until the leaves are slightly crushed and fragrant.
2. Fill the glass with crushed ice.
3. Pour the bourbon over the ice and stir until the glass is frosted on the outside.
4. Top up the glass with more crushed ice and garnish with a mint sprig. Serve with a straw.

Old Fashioned

Prep: 2 minutes – Cook: 5 minutes – Servings: 1
Calories: 140 – Fat 0g – Carbs: 2g – Fiber: 0g – Sugar: 2g – Protein 0g

The Old Fashioned is a classic cocktail that is made with whiskey, sugar, bitters, and a citrus twist. It is a simple yet delicious cocktail that is perfect for sipping on a chilly evening or enjoying as a nightcap.

Ingredients

- 2 ounces whiskey (rye or bourbon)
- 1 sugar cube or 1 teaspoon granulated sugar
- 2 dashes of Angostura bitters
- 1 orange peel or lemon twist
- Ice

Directions

1. Place the sugar cube or granulated sugar in an Old-Fashioned glass.
2. Add 2 dashes of Angostura bitters to the glass.
3. Use a muddler or the back of a spoon to muddle the sugar and bitters together until the sugar is dissolved.
4. Add a large ice cube (or a few small ones) to the glass.
5. Pour the whiskey over the ice and stir gently.
6. Use a vegetable peeler or knife to cut a strip of orange peel or a lemon twist.
7. Squeeze the orange peel or lemon twist over the drink to release the oils, then garnish the glass with the twist.

Appetizers

Deviled Eggs

Prep: 10 minutes – Cook: 25 minutes – Servings: 6
Calories: 90 – Fat 6g – Carbs: 1g – Fiber: 1g – Sugar: 1g – Protein 3g

Deviled eggs are a classic appetizer or side dish that is perfect for parties, picnics, or as a snack. They are hard-boiled eggs that have been halved, and the yolks are mixed with other ingredients such as mayonnaise, mustard, and spices to create a creamy filling.

Ingredients

- 6 large eggs
- ¼ cup mayonnaise
- 1 tablespoon yellow mustard
- ⅛ teaspoon black pepper
- Paprika, for garnish
- ⅛ teaspoon salt
- Chopped fresh chives, for garnish

Directions

1. Place the eggs in a large pot and cover with cold water.
2. Bring the water to a boil over high heat, then reduce the heat to low and simmer for 10-12 minutes.
3. Remove the pot from the heat and let the eggs cool for a few minutes in the water.
4. Drain the water and run cold water over the eggs to cool them completely.
5. Once the eggs are cool, carefully peel them and cut them in half lengthwise.
6. Remove the yolks and place them in a mixing bowl.
7. Mash the yolks with a fork until they are crumbly.
8. Add the mayonnaise, mustard, salt, and black pepper to the bowl and stir until the mixture is smooth.
9. Use a spoon or a piping bag to fill each egg white half with the yolk mixture.
10. Sprinkle the deviled eggs with paprika and chopped chives for garnish. Chill the deviled eggs in the refrigerator until ready to serve.

Oysters Rockefeller

Prep: 20 minutes – Cook: 20 minutes – Servings: 4
Calories: 200 – Fat 14g – Carbs: 7g – Fiber: 1g – Sugar: 1g – Protein 7g

Oysters Rockefeller is a classic dish made with oysters on the half shell that have been topped with a mixture of breadcrumbs, herbs, butter, and other ingredients, then baked or broiled until crispy and golden.

Ingredients

- 12 oysters, on the half shell
- ¼ cup unsalted butter, melted
- ½ cup breadcrumbs
- ¼ cup grated Parmesan cheese
- 1 tablespoon chopped shallot
- ¼ cup chopped parsley
- 1 tablespoon Pernod (an anise-flavored liqueur)
- ¼ cup chopped spinach
- Salt and pepper to taste
- Lemon wedges, for serving

Directions

1. Preheat your oven to 450 F.
2. Shuck the oysters and leave them on their half shell.
3. Arrange the oysters on a baking sheet.
4. In a mixing bowl, combine the breadcrumbs, butter, Parmesan cheese, parsley, spinach, shallot, Pernod, salt, and pepper.
5. Mix everything together until it forms a thick paste.
6. Spoon a generous dollop of the breadcrumb mixture on top of each oyster.
7. Place the baking sheet in the oven and bake for 8-10 minutes or until the topping is golden brown and crispy.
8. Remove the baking sheet from the oven and let the oysters cool for a few minutes.
9. Serve the Oysters Rockefeller hot with lemon wedges.

Shrimp Cocktail

Prep: 20 minutes – Cook: 35 minutes – Servings: 4
Calories: 144 – Fat 2g – Carbs: 12g – Fiber: 1g – Sugar: 9g – Protein 22g

Shrimp cocktail is a classic appetizer or hors d'oeuvre that typically consists of cooked, chilled shrimp served with a tangy cocktail sauce. The shrimp are often arranged on a bed of lettuce or other greens, and the cocktail sauce is usually made with ketchup, horseradish, Worcestershire sauce, lemon juice, and hot sauce

Ingredients

- 1-pound large shrimp, cooked and peeled, tails on
- ½ cup ketchup
- 1 tablespoon Worcestershire sauce
- 2 tablespoons prepared horseradish
- 1 tablespoon lemon juice
- Pepper and salt to taste
- ¼ teaspoon hot sauce (optional)
- Lemon wedges and fresh parsley for garnish

Directions

1. Rinse the cooked shrimp under cold water and pat dry with paper towels.
2. Arrange the shrimp on a platter or individual cocktail glasses.
3. In a small bowl, whisk together ketchup, horseradish, Worcestershire sauce, lemon juice, hot sauce, salt, and pepper.
4. Serve the cocktail sauce on the side or pour over the shrimp.
5. Garnish with lemon wedges and fresh parsley.
6. Chill in the refrigerator until ready to serve.

Waldorf Salad

Prep: 10 minutes – Cook: 35 minutes – Servings: 3
Calories: 314 – Fat 24g – Carbs: 20g – Fiber: 4g – Sugar: 14g – Protein 5g

Waldorf salad is a classic salad that originated in New York City in the late 1800s at the Waldorf Astoria Hotel. It is typically made with crisp apples, celery, grapes, and walnuts, mixed with a dressing made from mayonnaise, lemon juice, and sometimes sour cream or yogurt

Ingredients

- 2 medium apples, cored and chopped
- 1 cup chopped celery
- ½ cup walnuts, chopped
- 1 cup red seedless grapes, halved
- ¼ cup mayonnaise
- 2 tablespoons lemon juice
- Pepper & salt to taste
- 2 tablespoons plain yogurt
- Lettuce leaves for serving (optional)

Directions

1. In a large bowl, combine the chopped apples, celery, grapes, and walnuts.
2. In a small bowl, whisk together the mayonnaise, lemon juice, and yogurt.
3. Pour the dressing over the apple mixture and toss to coat.
4. Season with salt and pepper to taste.
5. Chill in the refrigerator for at least 30 minutes before serving.
6. Serve the salad on a bed of lettuce leaves, if desired.

Celery Victor

Prep: 10 minutes – Cook: 35 minutes – Servings: 2
Calories: 84 – Fat 7g – Carbs: 6g – Fiber: 2g – Sugar: 4g – Protein 1g

Celery Victor is a classic salad that features blanched celery stalks dressed with tangy vinaigrette.

Ingredients

- ½ cup white wine vinegar
- 8-10 celery stalks
- 1 tablespoon Dijon mustard
- ¼ cup chopped fresh parsley
- 1 tablespoon honey
- ¼ cup extra-virgin olive oil
- Pepper & salt to taste

Directions

1. Wash the celery stalks and trim the leaves and ends.
2. Bring a large pot of salted water to a boil.
3. Add the celery stalks and cook for 2-3 minutes until they are slightly tender but still crisp.
4. Drain the celery and immediately transfer to a bowl of ice water to stop the cooking process. Drain again and pat dry with paper towels.
5. In a small bowl, whisk together the white wine vinegar, olive oil, Dijon mustard, honey, and chopped parsley.
6. Season with salt and pepper to taste.
7. Pour the vinaigrette over the celery stalks and toss to coat.
8. Chill in the refrigerator for at least 30 minutes before serving.

Stuffed Mushrooms

Prep: 10 minutes – Cook: 35 minutes – Servings: 4
Calories: 60 – Fat 4g – Carbs: 4g – Fiber: 1g – Sugar: 1g – Protein 3g

Stuffed mushrooms are a delicious appetizer that can be served at parties, gatherings, or enjoyed as a snack.

Ingredients

- ½ cup Parmesan cheese, grated
- 20-25 mushrooms, medium-sized
- ½ cup seasoned breadcrumbs
- 3 garlic cloves, minced
- ¼ cup fresh parsley, chopped
- 3 tablespoons olive oil
- Pepper & salt to taste

Directions

1. Preheat the oven to 375 F.
2. Wash the mushrooms and remove the stems, setting them aside.
3. In a small bowl, combine the breadcrumbs, Parmesan cheese, parsley, garlic, and olive oil. Stir well to combine.
4. Season the mushroom caps with salt and pepper to taste.
5. Stuff each mushroom cap with the breadcrumb mixture, pressing down slightly to make sure the filling sticks.
6. Place the stuffed mushrooms on a baking sheet lined with parchment paper.
7. Bake until the mushrooms are tender, and the filling is golden brown, for 18-20 minutes.
8. Serve hot, garnished with additional chopped parsley if desired.

Clams Casino

Prep: 20 minutes – Cook: 25 minutes – Servings: 4
Calories: 134 – Fat 10g – Carbs: 7g – Fiber: 1g – Sugar: 1g – Protein 6g

Clams Casino is a classic appetizer dish made with clams, bacon, breadcrumbs, and various seasonings

Ingredients

- 4 slices of bacon
- 12-16 small clams
- ½ cup breadcrumbs
- 2 tablespoons Parmesan cheese, grated
- ¼ cup unsalted butter, melted
- 2 cloves garlic, minced
- Pepper & salt to taste
- 2 tablespoons fresh parsley, chopped
- Lemon wedges, for serving

Directions

1. Preheat the oven to 400 F.
2. Wash the clams and shuck them, setting them aside on the half shell.
3. In a skillet, cook the bacon until crispy. Remove the bacon from the pan and crumble it into small pieces.
4. In a small bowl, combine the breadcrumbs, Parmesan cheese, parsley, garlic, and crumbled bacon.
5. Add the melted butter to the breadcrumb mixture and stir well to combine.
6. Season the clams with salt and pepper to taste.
7. Spoon the breadcrumb mixture over each clam, pressing down slightly to make sure the filling sticks.
8. Place the clams on a baking sheet lined with parchment paper.
9. Bake for 10-12 minutes until the clams are cooked through and the filling is golden brown.
10. Serve hot, with lemon wedges for squeezing over the clams.

Lobster Newburg

Prep: 10 minutes – Cook: 25 minutes – Servings: 4
Calories: 634 – Fat 44g – Carbs: 22g – Fiber: 2g – Sugar: 9g – Protein 32g

Lobster Newburg is a classic dish made with lobster meat, butter, cream, and various seasonings.

Ingredients

- ½ cup unsalted butter
- 1-pound cooked lobster meat, chopped into bite-sized pieces
- ½ cup all-purpose flour
- 2 cups whole milk
- ½ cup heavy cream
- ¼ cup dry sherry
- Pepper & salt to taste
- ½ teaspoon paprika
- Toasted bread or puff pastry shells for serving (optional)

Directions

1. In a saucepan, melt the butter over medium heat.
2. Whisk in the flour and continue to whisk until the mixture turns golden brown.
3. Gradually whisk in the milk and heavy cream, stirring constantly to prevent lumps.
4. Add the sherry, paprika, salt, and pepper, and continue to stir until the mixture thickens.
5. Add the chopped lobster meat and cook for another 2-3 minutes, until the lobster is heated through.
6. Serve the Lobster Newburg hot, garnished with additional paprika if desired. You can also serve it over toasted bread or in puff pastry shells for a more elegant presentation.

Asparagus Vinaigrette

Prep: 10 minutes – Cook: 20 minutes – Servings: 4
Calories: 129 – Fat 12g – Carbs: 5g – Fiber: 2g – Sugar: 2g – Protein 3g

Asparagus vinaigrette is a simple, yet elegant dish made with steamed asparagus and a tangy vinaigrette dressing.

Ingredients

- 1 pound asparagus, tough ends trimmed
- 2 tablespoons white wine vinegar
- 1 tablespoon Dijon mustard
- ¼ cup extra-virgin olive oil
- Freshly ground black pepper & salt to taste

Optional Garnishes:
- chopped fresh parsley
- hard-boiled egg
- chopped chives

Directions

1. Fill a large pot with salted water and bring it to a boil.
2. Add the asparagus and cook for 3-5 minutes, until tender-crisp.
3. Drain the asparagus and transfer it to a serving platter.
4. In a small bowl, whisk together the white wine vinegar and Dijon mustard.
5. Gradually whisk in the olive oil until the dressing is emulsified.
6. Season the dressing with salt and pepper to taste.
7. Drizzle the dressing over the asparagus and toss to coat.
8. Garnish with hard-boiled egg, chopped fresh parsley, or chopped chives if desired.
9. Serve the asparagus vinaigrette at room temperature or chilled.

Tomato Aspic

Prep: 10 minutes – Cook: 4 hours & 20 minutes – Servings: 3
Calories: 47 – Fat 0g – Carbs: 7g – Fiber: 1g – Sugar: 4g – Protein 4g

Tomato aspic is a classic dish that consists of tomato juice and gelatin.

Ingredients

- 3 cups tomato juice
- Dash of hot sauce
- 2 tablespoons unflavored gelatin
- ½ teaspoon salt
- 2 tablespoons lemon juice

Optional Garnishes:
- Sliced hard-boiled eggs
- Mayonnaise
- Chopped fresh herbs
- Diced celery

Directions

1. In a large saucepan, heat the tomato juice until it is hot but not boiling.
2. In a small bowl, sprinkle the gelatin over the lemon juice and let it sit for a few minutes to soften.
3. Add the softened gelatin mixture to the hot tomato juice and whisk until the gelatin is completely dissolved.
4. Stir in the salt and hot sauce.
5. Pour the tomato mixture into a 4-cup mold or individual molds.
6. Chill the tomato aspic in the refrigerator for at least 4 hours, or until it is set.
7. To serve, unmold the tomato aspic onto a platter and garnish with mayonnaise, sliced hard-boiled eggs, diced celery, or chopped fresh herbs if desired.

Entrees

Chicken a la King

Prep: 20 minutes – Cook: 35 minutes – Servings: 4
Calories: 442 – Fat 34g – Carbs: 9g – Fiber: 1g – Sugar: 3g – Protein 24g

Chicken a la King is a classic dish that typically consists of diced chicken, mushrooms, and bell peppers in a creamy sauce, served over rice or toast.

Ingredients

- ½ cup diced onion
- 4 tablespoons butter
- ½ cup diced bell pepper
- 2 cups chicken broth
- ½ cup sliced mushrooms
- 1 cup heavy cream
- ¼ cup all-purpose flour
- 2 cups diced cooked chicken
- ¼ teaspoon black pepper
- ½ teaspoon salt

Optional Ingredients:
- Sliced pimientos
- Chopped fresh parsley

Directions

1. In a large skillet, melt the butter over medium heat.
2. Add the onion, bell pepper, and mushrooms to the skillet and cook until the vegetables are tender.
3. Sprinkle the flour over the vegetables and stir to coat.
4. Gradually add the chicken broth and cream to the skillet, stirring constantly to prevent lumps.
5. Bring the mixture to a boil, then reduce the heat and simmer until the sauce is thickened.
6. Stir in the diced chicken and season with salt and black pepper.
7. Cook for a few more minutes until the chicken is heated through.
8. Serve the chicken a la king over rice or toast, garnished with sliced pimientos and chopped fresh parsley if desired.

Beef Wellington

Prep: 20 minutes – Cook: 1 hour & 25 minutes – Servings: 4
Calories: 742 – Fat 54g – Carbs: 26g – Fiber: 2g – Sugar: 1g – Protein 36g

Beef Wellington is a classic British dish that consists of beef tenderloin coated in a mushroom and shallot mixture, wrapped in puff pastry, and baked until golden brown.

Ingredients

- 4 tablespoons unsalted butter
- ½ cup shallots, finely chopped
- 8 ounces mushrooms, finely chopped
- 1 beef tenderloin (2-pound), trimmed
- 2 tablespoons Dijon mustard
- 1 egg, beaten
- 2 sheets puff pastry, thawed
- ¼ cup dry sherry
- Freshly ground black pepper & salt to taste

Directions

1. Preheat the oven to 425 F.
2. Season the beef tenderloin with salt and pepper on all sides.
3. Melt 2 tablespoons of butter in a large skillet over medium-high heat.
4. Sear the beef tenderloin on all sides until browned, about 2-3 minutes per side.
5. Remove the beef from the skillet and set aside to cool.
6. In the same skillet, melt the remaining 2 tablespoons of butter over medium heat.
7. Add the shallots and cook until softened, about 2 minutes.
8. Add the mushrooms and cook until the liquid has evaporated, about 5-7 minutes.
9. Add the sherry and cook until the liquid has evaporated, about 2-3 minutes.
10. Remove the mushroom mixture from the heat and stir in the Dijon mustard.
11. Roll out the puff pastry on a lightly floured surface.
12. Place the beef tenderloin in the center of the pastry.
13. Spread the mushroom mixture over the top of the beef.
14. Fold the pastry over the beef and seal the edges with the beaten egg.
15. Transfer the beef Wellington to a baking sheet lined with parchment paper.
16. Brush the top of the pastry with the beaten egg.
17. Bake in the oven for 35-40 minutes, until the pastry is golden brown, and the beef is cooked to your desired doneness.
18. Remove from the oven, let rest for 10 minutes, and slice into portions.
19. Serve hot and enjoy your delicious beef Wellington.

Lobster Thermidor

Prep: 20 minutes – Cook: 35 minutes – Servings: 2
Calories: 534 – Fat 37g – Carbs: 5g – Fiber: 2g – Sugar: 2g – Protein 34

Lobster Thermidor is a classic French dish that typically consists of cooked lobster meat in a creamy sauce, flavored with mustard, white wine, and herbs, and served in the lobster shell.

Ingredients

- ¼ cup Dijon mustard
- 2 cooked lobsters, approximately 1 ½ to 2 pounds each
- ¼ cup brandy or cognac
- 4 tablespoons unsalted butter
- ¼ cup grated Parmesan cheese
- 1 shallot, minced
- ½ cup dry white wine
- 1 cup heavy cream
- ¼ cup fresh parsley, chopped
- Freshly ground black pepper & salt to taste

Directions

1. Preheat the oven to 375 F.
2. Cut the lobsters in half lengthwise, remove the meat from the claws and tails, and chop the meat into bite-sized pieces.
3. Melt the butter in a large skillet over medium heat.
4. Add the shallot and cook until softened, about 2 minutes.
5. Add the white wine and cognac and bring to a boil.
6. Add the heavy cream and mustard and whisk to combine.
7. Add the lobster meat to the skillet and stir to coat with the sauce.
8. Stir in the Parmesan cheese and parsley and season with salt and pepper to taste.
9. Transfer the lobster mixture to the lobster shells and place them on a baking sheet.
10. Bake in the oven for 10 to 15 minutes, until the sauce is bubbly and lightly browned on top.
11. Serve hot and enjoy your delicious lobster Thermidor.

Sole Veronique

Prep: 10 minutes – Cook: 45 minutes – Servings: 4
Calories: 414 – Fat 24g – Carbs: 9g – Fiber: 1g – Sugar: 4g – Protein 26g

Sole Veronique is a classic French dish that consists of sautéed sole fillets served with a sauce made from white wine, cream, and grapes.

Ingredients

- 4 sole fillets
- ½ cup dry white wine
- All-purpose flour, for dredging
- ½ cup seedless green grapes, halved
- 4 tablespoons unsalted butter
- ½ cup heavy cream
- Freshly ground black pepper and salt to taste

Directions

1. Season the sole fillets with salt and pepper on both sides.
2. Dredge the fillets in flour, shaking off any excess.
3. Melt 2 tablespoons of butter in a large skillet over medium-high heat.
4. Add the sole fillets to the skillet and cook for 2-3 minutes per side, until golden brown and cooked through.
5. Remove the sole fillets from the skillet and set aside.
6. Add the white wine to the skillet and cook, stirring occasionally, until the wine has reduced by half.
7. Add the heavy cream to the skillet and cook, stirring occasionally, until the sauce has thickened and coats the back of a spoon.
8. Stir in the grapes and remaining 2 tablespoons of butter.
9. Return the sole fillets to the skillet and spoon the sauce over the top.
10. Serve hot and enjoy your delicious Sole Veronique.

Chicken Tetrazzini

Prep: 10 minutes – Cook: 55 minutes – Servings: 4
Calories: 744 – Fat 42g – Carbs: 64g – Fiber: 3g – Sugar: 5g – Protein 31g

Chicken Tetrazzini is a classic Italian American dish that combines cooked spaghetti or fettuccine noodles with a creamy sauce made from chicken broth, heavy cream, and Parmesan cheese, along with cooked chicken and mushrooms.

Ingredients

- 1 pound spaghetti or fettuccine noodles
- ½ cup all-purpose flour
- 4 cups chicken broth
- ½ cup unsalted butter
- 2 cups heavy cream
- ½ cup grated Parmesan cheese
- 1 teaspoon garlic powder
- 2 cups cooked and shredded chicken
- 1 teaspoon onion powder
- 2 cups sliced mushrooms
- Pepper & salt and, to taste
- ¼ cup chopped fresh parsley

Directions

1. Preheat the oven to 350 F. Grease a 9x13 inch baking dish.
2. Cook the spaghetti or fettuccine noodles according to package instructions. Drain and set aside.
3. In a large saucepan, melt the butter over medium heat.
4. Add the flour and whisk until smooth and bubbly, about 1-2 minutes.
5. Gradually add the chicken broth and whisk until the mixture is smooth.
6. Bring the mixture to a boil, then reduce the heat to low and simmer for 5 minutes, stirring frequently.
7. Add the heavy cream, Parmesan cheese, garlic powder, onion powder, salt, and pepper. Stir to combine.
8. Add the cooked chicken and sliced mushrooms to the sauce and stir to combine.
9. Add the cooked noodles to the sauce and toss to coat.
10. Pour the mixture into the prepared baking dish.
11. Bake until bubbly and golden brown, for 25-30 minutes.
12. Remove from the oven and let cool for a few minutes before serving. Garnish with chopped parsley and enjoy your delicious Chicken Tetrazzini.

Oysters Bienville

Prep: 20 minutes – Cook: 50 minutes – Servings: 6
Calories: 522 – Fat 34g – Carbs: 24g – Fiber: 1g – Sugar: 5g – Protein 26g

Oysters Bienville is a classic New Orleans dish that consists of oysters baked with a rich and creamy filling made from a mixture of butter, flour, milk, cream, and various seasonings.

Ingredients

- 24 oysters, shucked
- ½ cup chopped onions
- 4 tablespoons unsalted butter
- ½ cup heavy cream
- 4 tablespoons all-purpose flour
- ½ cup chopped green bell pepper
- 2 garlic cloves, minced
- 1 cup milk
- ½ cup Parmesan cheese, grated
- 1 tablespoon Worcestershire sauce
- 1 teaspoon hot sauce
- ¼ teaspoon cayenne pepper
- ½ cup plain breadcrumbs
- ¼ teaspoon black pepper
- ½ cup chopped celery
- 2 tablespoons chopped fresh parsley
- ½ teaspoon salt

Directions

1. Preheat the oven to 375 F.
2. In a large saucepan, melt the butter over medium heat.
3. Add the flour and whisk until smooth and bubbly, about 1-2 minutes.
4. Add the onions, celery, bell pepper, and garlic, and cook until the vegetables are soft and translucent, about 5-7 minutes.
5. Gradually add the milk and heavy cream, whisking constantly to prevent lumps.
6. Bring the mixture to a boil, then reduce the heat to low and simmer for 5 minutes, stirring frequently.
7. Add the Parmesan cheese, Worcestershire sauce, hot sauce, salt, cayenne pepper, and black pepper. Stir to combine.
8. Remove the saucepan from the heat and let the mixture cool for a few minutes.
9. Arrange the shucked oysters in a single layer in a baking dish.
10. Pour the sauce over the oysters, covering each one completely.
11. In a small bowl, mix together the breadcrumbs and chopped parsley.
12. Sprinkle the bread crumb mixture evenly over the top of the oysters.
13. Bake for 15-20 minutes, or until the topping is golden brown and the oysters are cooked through.
14. Remove from the oven and let cool for a few minutes before serving.

Duck a l'Orange

Prep: 20 minutes – Cook: 1 hour & 50 minutes – Servings: 8
Calories: 444 – Fat 40g – Carbs: 20g – Fiber: 2g – Sugar: 20g – Protein 29g

Duck à l'Orange is a classic French dish that consists of roasted duck with a tangy orange sauce.

Ingredients

- 2 oranges
- 1 whole duck (approximately 4-5 pounds)
- 2 cups chicken broth
- ¼ cup orange liqueur (such as Grand Marnier)
- 2 tablespoons unsalted butter
- ¼ cup sugar
- 2 tablespoons all-purpose flour
- Pepper & salt

Directions

1. Preheat the oven to 350 F.
2. Rinse the duck inside and out with cold water and pat dry with paper towels.
3. Season the duck inside and out with salt and pepper.
4. Cut one of the oranges in half and squeeze the juice into a small bowl. Set aside.
5. Cut the other orange into thin slices and set aside.
6. Place the duck, breast side up, on a rack in a roasting pan.
7. Roast the duck in the preheated oven for 1 ½ to 2 hours, or until the internal temperature reaches 165 F.
8. While the duck is roasting, prepare the orange sauce. In a small saucepan, combine the chicken broth, orange liqueur, sugar, and orange juice. Bring to a boil over medium-high heat, stirring occasionally, until the sugar has dissolved.
9. In a separate small saucepan, melt the butter over medium heat. Add the flour and whisk until smooth and bubbly, about 1-2 minutes.
10. Gradually add the chicken broth mixture to the butter mixture, whisking constantly to prevent lumps.
11. Bring the mixture to a boil, then reduce the heat to low and simmer for 5-7 minutes, stirring frequently, until the sauce has thickened.
12. When the duck is done, remove it from the oven and let it rest for 10 minutes before carving.
13. Arrange the duck slices on a serving platter and pour the orange sauce over the top.
14. Garnish with the orange slices and serve hot.

Eggs Benedict

Prep: 25 minutes – Cook: 45 minutes – Servings: 4
Calories: 694 – Fat 40g – Carbs: 39g – Fiber: 4g – Sugar: 4g – Protein 34g

Eggs Benedict is a classic breakfast dish consisting of a toasted English muffin topped with Canadian bacon or ham, a poached egg, and hollandaise sauce.

Ingredients

- 8 slices Canadian bacon or ham
- 4 English muffins, split and toasted
- 1 tablespoon white vinegar
- 8 large eggs
- ½ cup unsalted butter
- 3 large egg yolks
- Salt and pepper, to taste
- 1 tablespoon fresh lemon juice
- Chopped fresh parsley, for garnish (optional)

Directions

1. Preheat the oven to 200 F.
2. Place the toasted English muffin halves on a baking sheet and top each half with a slice of Canadian bacon or ham. Keep warm in the oven while you prepare the eggs and hollandaise sauce.
3. To poach the eggs, fill a large, deep skillet with approximately 2" of water. Add the white vinegar and bring the water to a gentle simmer over medium heat.
4. Crack each egg into a small bowl or ramekin, being careful not to break the yolks.
5. Using a spoon, create a gentle whirlpool in the simmering water. Carefully slide each egg into the water, one at a time. Cook for about 3-4 minutes, or until the whites are set and the yolks are still runny.
6. Use a slotted spoon to remove the poached eggs from the water and place them on a paper towel-lined plate to drain excess water.
7. To make the hollandaise sauce, melt the butter in a small saucepan over medium-low heat. In a separate bowl, whisk together the egg yolks and lemon juice until pale and thick.
8. Gradually pour the melted butter into the egg yolk mixture, whisking constantly, until the sauce is thick and creamy. Season with salt and pepper, to taste.
9. To assemble the Eggs Benedict, place two English muffin halves with Canadian bacon on each plate. Top each half with a poached egg. Spoon hollandaise sauce over the top of each egg.
10. Garnish with chopped fresh parsley, if desired.
11. Serve hot and enjoy your delicious Eggs Benedict.

Veal Oscar

Prep: 25 minutes – Cook: 35 minutes – Servings: 4
Calories: 534 – Fat 34g – Carbs: 14g – Fiber: 2g – Sugar: 2g – Protein 34g

Veal Oscar is a classic dish that features veal medallions topped with asparagus, crab meat, and a rich hollandaise sauce.

Ingredients

- ½ pound asparagus, trimmed and blanched
- 4 veal medallions, about 4 ounces each
- ½ pound lump crab meat
- 4 tablespoons unsalted butter
- ¼ cup all-purpose flour
- Freshly ground black pepper & salt to taste
- ½ cup hollandaise sauce (store-bought or homemade)
- Lemon wedges, for serving

Directions

1. Season the veal medallions with salt and pepper on both sides.
2. Dredge the veal medallions in flour, shaking off any excess.
3. Melt 2 tablespoons of butter in a large skillet over medium-high heat.
4. Add the veal medallions to the skillet and cook for 2-3 minutes per side, until golden brown and cooked through.
5. Remove the veal medallions from the skillet and set aside.
6. In the same skillet, melt the remaining 2 tablespoons of butter over medium heat.
7. Add the blanched asparagus to the skillet and cook for 2-3 minutes, until tender.
8. Add the lump crab meat to the skillet and cook for 1-2 minutes, until heated through.
9. To serve, place a veal medallion on each plate and top with the asparagus and crab meat mixture.
10. Spoon the hollandaise sauce over the top and garnish with lemon wedges.
11. Serve hot and enjoy your delicious Veal Oscar.

Steak Diane

Prep: 20 minutes – Cook: 45 minutes – Servings: 4
Calories: 494 – Fat 32g – Carbs: 36g – Fiber: 3g – Sugar: 4g – Protein 34g

Steak Diane is a classic dish that is usually made with a pan-fried beefsteak, served with a rich and creamy sauce made with mushrooms, brandy, and cream.

Ingredients

- 4 beef tenderloin steaks, approximately 1" thick
- 1 shallot, minced
- ¼ cup all-purpose flour
- 2 tablespoons unsalted butter
- ¼ cup brandy
- 1 cup sliced mushrooms
- ¼ cup heavy cream
- Salt and freshly ground black pepper
- ½ cup beef broth
- 2 tablespoons vegetable oil
- 1 tablespoon chopped fresh parsley

Directions

1. Preheat a large skillet over medium-high heat. Season the steaks with salt and pepper. Dredge them in the flour, shaking off any excess.
2. Add the butter and vegetable oil to the skillet. When the butter has melted and the oil is hot, add the steaks and cook for 2-3 minutes on each side, until browned and cooked to your desired level of doneness.
3. Remove the steaks from the skillet and set them aside on a plate. Add the shallot and mushrooms to the skillet and cook for 2-3 minutes, until softened. Add the brandy to the skillet and cook until it has evaporated. Add the beef broth to the skillet and bring to a boil. Reduce the heat to low and simmer for 3-4 minutes.
4. Add the heavy cream to the skillet and stir to combine. Cook for 1-2 minutes, until the sauce has thickened slightly. Return the steaks to the skillet and coat them with the sauce. Sprinkle with chopped parsley and serve hot.

Coq au Vin

Prep: 20 minutes – Cook: 2 hours & 35 minutes – Servings: 4
Calories: 494 – Fat 27g – Carbs: 10g – Fiber: 2g – Sugar: 3g – Protein 37g

Coq au Vin is a classic French dish that translates to "rooster in wine." The dish originated in the Burgundy region of France and is traditionally made with an older rooster, which requires long and slow cooking to become tender.

Ingredients

- 4 chicken thighs
- 6 slices of bacon, chopped
- 2 tablespoons flour
- 4 chicken drumsticks
- 2 garlic cloves, minced
- 1 large onion, chopped
- 2 cups dry red wine
- 1 cup chicken broth
- 2 tablespoons tomato paste
- 1 teaspoon dried thyme
- 2 tablespoons butter
- Pepper & salt to taste
- 2 cups sliced mushrooms
- Chopped fresh parsley, for garnish

Directions

1. In a large bowl, combine the chicken, red wine, and thyme. Cover and refrigerate for at least 4 hours, or overnight.
2. In a large Dutch oven or heavy pot, cook the bacon over medium heat until crisp. Remove the bacon with a slotted spoon and set aside.
3. In the same pot, brown the chicken on both sides, about 8 minutes total. Remove the chicken from the pot and set aside.
4. Add the onion and garlic to the pot and cook until softened, about 5 minutes.
5. Add the mushrooms and cook until browned, about 5 minutes.
6. Sprinkle the flour over the vegetables and cook for 1 minute, stirring constantly.
7. Add the tomato paste, chicken broth, and reserved wine marinade to the pot. Bring to a simmer.
8. Return the chicken to the pot and add the bacon. Cover and simmer over low heat for 1 ½ to 2 hours, or until the chicken is cooked through and tender.
9. Remove the chicken from the pot and set aside. Bring the sauce to a boil and cook until thickened, about 10 minutes.
10. Stir in the butter until melted and smooth. Season with salt and pepper to taste.
11. Serve the chicken with the sauce and garnish with chopped fresh parsley.

Salmon Mousse

Prep: 20 minutes – Cook: 2 hours & 35 minutes – Servings: 4
Calories: 164 – Fat 12g – Carbs: 2g – Fiber: 1g – Sugar: 1g – Protein 10g

Salmon mousse is a delicious and elegant dish that can be served as an appetizer or a light meal

Ingredients

- 12 ounces cooked salmon, skin and bones removed
- ½ cup heavy cream
- 4 ounces cream cheese, softened
- 1 tablespoon Dijon mustard
- 2 tablespoons fresh lemon juice
- Pepper & salt to taste
- ¼ cup chopped fresh dill
- Toasted bread or crackers, for serving

Directions

1. In a food processor, pulse the cooked salmon until it is finely chopped.
2. Add the cream cheese, heavy cream, lemon juice, and Dijon mustard to the food processor. Pulse until the mixture is smooth and creamy.
3. Add the chopped fresh dill and pulse a few times to combine. Season with salt and pepper to taste.
4. Transfer the salmon mousse to a serving dish and chill in the refrigerator for at least 2 hours, or overnight. Serve the salmon mousse with toasted bread or crackers.

Tournedos Rossini

Prep: 20 minutes – Cook: 55 minutes – Servings: 4
Calories: 694 – Fat 40g – Carbs: 39g – Fiber: 4g – Sugar: 4g – Protein 34g

Tournedos Rossini is a classic French dish that consists of a tenderloin steak (tournedos) topped with foie gras and truffles, served with a sauce made from Madeira wine. The dish is named after the Italian composer Gioachino Rossini, who was a lover of fine cuisine.

Ingredients

- 4 beef tenderloin steaks, 6-8 ounces each
- 1 cup Madeira wine
- 4 slices of foie gras, about 2 ounces each
- 1 cup beef stock
- 2 shallots, finely chopped
- 4 slices of black truffle, about 1 ounce each
- Salt and pepper to taste
- 2 tablespoons butter
- Olive oil for cooking

Directions

1. Preheat the oven to 400 F.
2. Season the steaks with salt and pepper on both sides. Heat a large skillet over high heat and add the olive oil. Add the steaks and cook for 3-4 minutes on each side until browned. Transfer the steaks to a baking sheet and bake until they reach your desired doneness, for 5-7 minutes for medium-rare.
3. While the steaks are cooking, prepare the sauce. In the same skillet over medium-high heat, add the butter and sauté the shallots until they are translucent, about 2 minutes. Add the Madeira wine and beef stock and bring to a boil. Reduce the heat and let it simmer until the sauce thickens, for 15-20 minutes.
4. In a separate pan, sear the foie gras slices and truffle slices for about a minute on each side. To assemble the dish, place each steak on a plate and top with a slice of foie gras and a slice of truffle. Drizzle the sauce over the top and serve immediately.

Pork Tenderloin with Apples

Prep: 20 minutes – Cook: 50 minutes – Servings: 4
Calories: 140 – Fat 3g – Carbs: 2g – Fiber: 2g – Sugar: 1g – Protein 22g

Pork tenderloin with apples is a classic dish that combines the sweet and savory flavors of pork and apples.

Ingredients

- 1 ½ to 2 pounds pork tenderloin
- 2 tablespoons olive oil
- ¼ teaspoon black pepper
- 2 tablespoons butter
- 1 teaspoon dried thyme
- 2 large apples, cored and sliced
- ½ cup apple cider
- 1 large onion, thinly sliced
- ½ cup chicken broth
- 2 garlic cloves, minced
- ½ teaspoon salt
- ¼ cup heavy cream (optional)

Directions

1. Preheat the oven to 400 F.
2. In a small bowl, combine the olive oil, thyme, salt, and pepper. Rub the mixture all over the pork tenderloin.
3. Heat a large oven-safe skillet over medium-high heat. Add the pork tenderloin and cook for 2-3 minutes on each side until browned. Transfer the skillet to the oven and bake for 15-20 minutes or until the internal temperature of the pork reaches 145 F.
4. While the pork is cooking, melt the butter in a separate skillet over medium heat. Add the apples and onion and cook for 5-7 minutes or until they are softened and lightly browned. Add the garlic and cook for an additional minute.
5. Add the chicken broth and apple cider to the skillet with the apples and onion and bring to a simmer. Cook for 10-15 minutes or until the liquid is reduced and thickened.
6. Stir in the heavy cream to the apple mixture and simmer for 2 minutes.
7. To serve, slice the pork and spoon the apple mixture over the top.

Grilled Lamb Chops with Mint Jelly

Prep: 20 minutes – Cook: 50 minutes – Servings: 8
Calories: 230 – Fat 14g – Carbs: 7g – Fiber: 1g – Sugar: 2g – Protein 23g

Grilled lamb chops with mint jelly are a classic and flavorful dish that is perfect for a special occasion or a fancy dinner party

Ingredients

- 2 tablespoons fresh rosemary, chopped
- 8 lamb chops
- 2 garlic cloves, minced
- ½ cup mint jelly
- 2 tablespoons red wine vinegar
- 1 tablespoon Dijon mustard
- 2 tablespoons olive oil
- Pepper & salt, to taste

Directions

1. Preheat a grill or grill pan to medium-high heat.
2. In a small bowl, mix together the olive oil, garlic, and rosemary. Rub the mixture all over the lamb chops, then season with salt and pepper to taste.
3. Place the lamb chops on the grill and cook for 3-4 minutes per side for medium-rare, or until they reach your desired level of doneness.
4. While the lamb chops are cooking, make the mint jelly sauce. In a small saucepan, melt the mint jelly over medium heat. Stir in the red wine vinegar and Dijon mustard and whisk until well combined.
5. When the lamb chops are done, remove them from the grill and let them rest for a few minutes.
6. Serve the lamb chops with the mint jelly sauce drizzled over the top.

Filet Mignon with Béarnaise Sauce

Prep: 10 minutes – Cook: 45 minutes – Servings: 4
Calories: 320 – Fat 21g – Carbs: 14g – Fiber: 2g – Sugar: 3g – Protein 31g

Filet mignon with béarnaise sauce is a classic and elegant dish that is perfect for a special occasion or a fancy dinner party.

Ingredients

- 4 filet mignon steaks, approximately 6 ounces each
- 1 tablespoon white wine vinegar
- 4 egg yolks
- ½ cup unsalted butter, melted and cooled
- 1 tablespoon fresh tarragon, chopped
- 2 tablespoons olive oil
- Pepper & salt, to taste
- 1 tablespoon water
- Lemon juice, to taste

Directions

1. Preheat the oven to 400 F.
2. Heat a large skillet over medium-high heat. Add the olive oil.
3. Season the filet mignon steaks with salt and pepper to taste. Add them to the skillet and cook for 3-4 minutes per side, or until they are browned and seared on both sides.
4. Transfer the skillet to the oven and bake for 8-10 minutes for medium-rare, or until they reach your desired level of doneness.
5. While the filet mignon is cooking, make the béarnaise sauce. In a small saucepan, whisk together the egg yolks, water, and white wine vinegar. Place the saucepan over low heat and whisk constantly until the mixture thickens and becomes frothy.
6. Remove the saucepan from the heat and whisk in the tarragon and melted butter. Season with salt, pepper, and lemon juice to taste.
7. When the filet mignon is done, remove it from the oven and let it rest for a few minutes. Serve the filet mignon with the béarnaise sauce spooned over the top.

Corned Beef and Cabbage

Prep: 30 minutes – Cook: 3 hours & 50 minutes – Servings: 8
Calories: 214 – Fat 14g – Carbs: 19g – Fiber: 2g – Sugar: 2g – Protein 16g

Corned beef and cabbage are a traditional Irish American dish that is often served on St. Patrick's Day

Ingredients

- 3-4 pounds corned beef brisket
- 1 head green cabbage, cored and cut into wedges
- 5 large carrots, peeled and cut into 3-inch pieces
- 1 onion, peeled and cut into wedges
- 4 cloves garlic, minced
- 1 teaspoon whole black peppercorns
- 2 bay leaves
- Water
- 10 small red potatoes, washed and halved
- Salt and pepper, to taste

Directions

1. Rinse the corned beef brisket under cold running water to remove any excess salt. Place the brisket in a large pot or Dutch oven and add enough water to cover it by about 2 inches.
2. Add the onion, garlic, bay leaves, and whole black peppercorns to the pot. Bring the water to a boil over high heat, then reduce the heat to low and cover the pot.
3. Simmer the corned beef for about 3 hours, or until it is tender and can be easily pierced with a fork.
4. Add the potatoes and carrots to the pot and continue to simmer for another 20-30 minutes, or until the vegetables are tender.
5. Add the cabbage to the pot and simmer for another 10-15 minutes, or until the cabbage is tender.
6. Use a slotted spoon to transfer the corned beef and vegetables to a serving platter. Season with salt and pepper to taste.
7. Let the corned beef rest for a few minutes before slicing it against the grain. Serve the sliced corned beef and vegetables hot, garnished with fresh parsley if desired.

Lobster à l'Américaine

Prep: 20 minutes – Cook: 50 minutes – Servings: 6
Calories: 90 – Fat 1g – Carbs: 1g – Fiber: 2g – Sugar: 2g – Protein 16g

Lobster à l'Américaine is a classic French seafood dish that features lobster cooked in a tomato-based sauce flavored with brandy and herbs.

Ingredients

- 1 can (28 ounces) crushed tomatoes
- 2 live lobsters, approximately 1 to 1.5 pounds each
- 1 onion, finely chopped
- 2 tablespoons butter
- ¼ cup brandy or cognac
- 2 cloves garlic, minced
- Salt and pepper, to taste
- ½ cup heavy cream
- 1 bay leaf
- ½ teaspoon dried thyme
- Fresh parsley, chopped, for garnish
- ½ teaspoon dried oregano

Directions

1. Bring a large pot of salted water to a boil over high heat. Add the live lobsters and cook for about 8-10 minutes, or until they turn bright red, and the meat is cooked through. Remove the lobsters from the pot and let them cool slightly.
2. Remove the meat from the lobsters, discarding the shells and any internal organs. Cut the meat into bite-sized pieces and set aside.
3. In a large skillet or Dutch oven, melt the butter over medium-high heat. Add the onion and garlic and sauté for about 5 minutes, or until they are soft and translucent.
4. Add the brandy or cognac to the skillet and cook for 2-3 minutes, or until it has reduced by half.
5. Add the crushed tomatoes, bay leaf, thyme, oregano, salt, and pepper to the skillet. Stir to combine.
6. Reduce the heat to low and let the sauce simmer for 15-20 minutes, or until it has thickened, and the flavors have melded together.
7. Add the lobster meat to the skillet and stir to coat it with the sauce. Pour in the heavy cream and stir to combine.
8. Cook the lobster and sauce over low heat for 5-10 minutes, or until the lobster is heated through and the sauce has thickened to your liking.
9. Serve the lobster à l'Américaine hot, garnished with fresh parsley.

Pot-au-Feu

Prep: 20 minutes – Cook: 3 hours & 45 minutes – Servings: 9
Calories: 700 – Fat 24g – Carbs: 70g – Fiber: 4g – Sugar: 6g – Protein 34g

Pot-au-Feu is a traditional French beef stew that is made with various cuts of beef, vegetables, and spices.

Ingredients

- 2-3 pounds beef (preferably a mix of beef brisket, bone-in beef shank, and beef marrow bones)
- 1-pound carrots, peeled and cut into chunks
- 2 onions, peeled and quartered
- 1-pound turnips, peeled and cut into chunks
- 2 celery stalks, cut into chunks
- 1-pound potatoes, peeled and quartered
- 2 garlic cloves, peeled
- 10-12 black peppercorns
- 2 carrots, peeled and cut into chunks
- Salt, to taste
- Fresh parsley, chopped, for garnish
- 2 bay leaves

Directions

1. In a large stockpot, add the beef, onions, carrots, celery, garlic, bay leaves, peppercorns, and salt. Cover the ingredients with cold water and bring to a boil over high heat.
2. Once the water is boiling, reduce the heat to low and let the stew simmer for 2-3 hours, or until the beef is tender and the vegetables are cooked through.
3. Skim off any foam that rises to the surface of the stew during the cooking process.
4. Remove the beef from the pot and let it rest for a few minutes before slicing it into thick pieces.
5. Strain the vegetables and spices from the stew, reserving the cooking liquid.
6. In a separate pot, add the potatoes, turnips, and carrots to the reserved cooking liquid and bring to a boil. Let the vegetables cook for 10-15 minutes, or until they are tender.
7. To serve, place a few slices of beef in each bowl and top with the cooked vegetables. Ladle some of the cooking liquid over the top of the stew.
8. Garnish with fresh chopped parsley and serve hot.

Chicken Marengo

Prep: 20 minutes – Cook: 50 minutes – Servings: 4
Calories: 364 – Fat 14g – Carbs: 19g – Fiber: 2g – Sugar: 3g – Protein 19g

Chicken Marengo is a classic French dish that was created to celebrate Napoleon's victory at the Battle of Marengo. It typically consists of sautéed chicken pieces served in a tomato-based sauce with mushrooms and olives.

Ingredients

- 1 bay leaf
- 4 chicken thighs, bone-in and skin-on
- 1 can (14.5 ounces) diced tomatoes
- 2 garlic cloves, minced
- ½ cup white wine
- 1 cup chicken broth
- 8 ounces mushrooms, sliced
- 1 onion, chopped
- ½ cup pitted green olives
- Chopped parsley, for garnish
- 1 tablespoon tomato paste
- 2 tablespoons olive oil
- 1 teaspoon dried thyme
- Salt and pepper, to taste

Directions

1. Season the chicken thighs with salt and pepper.
2. In a large skillet, heat the olive oil over medium-high heat. Add the chicken thighs and cook for 6-7 minutes per side, or until browned and crispy. Remove the chicken from the skillet and set aside.
3. In the same skillet, add the onion and garlic and cook for 2-3 minutes, or until softened.
4. Add the white wine to the skillet and scrape the browned bits from the bottom of the pan. Let the wine cook for 2-3 minutes, or until it has reduced by half.
5. Add the diced tomatoes, chicken broth, tomato paste, thyme, and bay leaf to the skillet. Stir to combine and bring the mixture to a simmer.
6. Return the chicken thighs to the skillet and let them simmer in the sauce for 20-25 minutes, or until they are cooked through.
7. Add the sliced mushrooms and olives to the skillet and let them cook for an additional 5-7 minutes, or until the mushrooms are tender.
8. To serve, remove the bay leaf and spoon the chicken and sauce onto plates. Garnish with chopped parsley and serve hot.

Seafood Newburg

Prep: 20 minutes – Cook: 45 minutes – Servings: 4
Calories: 204 – Fat 4g – Carbs: 2g – Fiber: 1g – Sugar: 1g – Protein 16g

Seafood Newburg is a classic American dish made with a rich, creamy sauce and a variety of seafood, usually including shrimp, lobster, or crab.

Ingredients

- 1 pounds mixed seafood (shrimp, lobster, crab), cooked and chopped
- 4 tablespoons butter
- ¼ cup all-purpose flour
- 1 ½ cups milk
- ½ cup heavy cream
- 4 egg yolks
- ¼ teaspoon nutmeg
- 2 tablespoons fresh parsley, chopped
- ¼ cup dry sherry
- Salt and pepper, to taste

Directions

1. Melt the butter in a large saucepan over medium heat.
2. Add the flour and whisk until the mixture is smooth and bubbling, about 1-2 minutes.
3. Slowly pour in the milk, whisking constantly to avoid any lumps.
4. Add the heavy cream, sherry, nutmeg, salt, and pepper to the saucepan. Stir to combine.
5. Cook the sauce over medium heat for 5-10 minutes, or until it has thickened and coats the back of a spoon.
6. In a small bowl, whisk the egg yolks until they are smooth.
7. Slowly pour ½ cup of the hot sauce into the egg yolks, whisking constantly to temper the yolks and prevent them from curdling.
8. Pour the egg yolk mixture back into the saucepan, whisking constantly.
9. Add the cooked seafood to the sauce and stir to combine.
10. Cook the seafood and sauce over low heat for 5-10 minutes, or until the seafood is heated through and the sauce is thick and creamy.
11. Serve the Seafood Newburg hot, garnished with fresh parsley.

Veal Piccata

Prep: 20 minutes – Cook: 35 minutes – Servings: 4
Calories: 454 – Fat 24g – Carbs: 19g – Fiber: 2g – Sugar: 1g – Protein 39g

Veal Piccata is an Italian American dish that consists of thinly sliced veal scaloppine that is sautéed and served with a tangy lemon-caper sauce.

Ingredients

- 4 veal scaloppine (about 1 pound)
- ½ cup all-purpose flour
- 4 tablespoons unsalted butter, divided
- ½ cup dry white wine
- 2 tablespoons capers, drained
- Lemon wedges, for serving
- ½ cup chicken broth
- 2 tablespoons olive oil
- Salt and pepper, to taste
- 2 tablespoons fresh lemon juice
- Chopped parsley, for garnish

Directions

1. Season the veal scaloppine with salt and pepper, then dredge them in the flour, shaking off any excess.
2. In a large skillet, melt 2 tablespoons of butter and the olive oil over medium-high heat. When the butter is melted and hot, add the veal scaloppine and cook for 2-3 minutes per side, or until golden brown. Remove the veal from the skillet and set aside.
3. Add the white wine to the skillet and cook for 1-2 minutes, or until the wine has reduced by half. Add the chicken broth, lemon juice, and capers to the skillet. Stir to combine and bring the mixture to a simmer.
4. Add the remaining 2 tablespoons of butter to the skillet and stir until it has melted, and the sauce has thickened slightly.
5. Return the veal scaloppine to the skillet and let them cook in the sauce for 2-3 minutes, or until heated through.
6. To serve, remove the veal scaloppine from the skillet and spoon the sauce over them. Garnish with chopped parsley and serve with lemon wedges.

Stuffed Bell Peppers

Prep: 30 minutes – Cook: 55 minutes – Servings: 4
Calories: 400 – Fat 20g – Carbs: 30g – Fiber: 6g – Sugar: 3g – Protein 24g

Stuffed bell peppers are a delicious and healthy meal option that can be made with a variety of ingredients.

Ingredients

- 1 can diced tomatoes (14.5 ounces)
- 1 pound ground beef
- 4 bell peppers
- 1 cup cooked rice
- 1 small onion, diced
- 2 garlic cloves, minced
- 1 teaspoon dried oregano
- Salt and pepper, to taste
- 1 teaspoon dried basil
- Shredded cheese, for topping, optional

Directions

1. Preheat the oven to 375 F.
2. Cut off the tops of the bell peppers and remove the seeds and membranes. Set aside.
3. In a large skillet, brown the ground beef over medium heat. Drain any excess fat.
4. Add the diced onion and garlic to the skillet and cook until the onion is translucent.
5. Add the cooked rice, diced tomatoes, oregano, basil, salt, and pepper to the skillet. Stir to combine.
6. Stuff the bell peppers with the beef and rice mixture, packing it down tightly.
7. Place the stuffed peppers in a baking dish and cover with foil.
8. Bake in the preheated oven for 30 minutes.
9. Remove the foil and sprinkle shredded cheese over the top of each pepper.
10. Bake for an 10-15 minutes more, or until cheese is melted and bubbly.
11. Serve the stuffed peppers hot, garnished with chopped parsley if desired.

Chicken Cordon Bleu

Prep: 20 minutes – Cook: 50 minutes – Servings: 4
Calories: 444 – Fat 24g – Carbs: 19g – Fiber: 2g – Sugar: 2g – Protein 34g

Chicken Cordon Bleu is a delicious and classic French dish that can be made easily at home.

Ingredients

- 4 boneless, skinless chicken breasts
- ½ cup all-purpose flour
- 4 slices of ham
- 2 eggs, beaten
- Salt and pepper, to taste
- 1 cup panko breadcrumbs
- 4 slices of Swiss cheese
- Olive oil or cooking spray

Directions

1. Preheat the oven to 375 F. Place a chicken breast between two sheets of plastic wrap and pound it with a meat mallet until it is approximately ¼" thick. Repeat with the remaining chicken breasts.
2. Place a slice of ham and a slice of Swiss cheese on each chicken breast and roll up tightly.
3. Secure the chicken breasts with toothpicks or kitchen twine.
4. Place the flour in a shallow dish and season with salt and pepper.
5. Place the beaten eggs in another shallow dish.
6. Place the panko breadcrumbs in a third shallow dish.
7. Coat each chicken roll in the flour, shaking off any excess.
8. Dip each chicken roll into the beaten eggs, then coat with the panko breadcrumbs.
9. Heat a large skillet over medium-high heat and add enough olive oil to coat the bottom of the pan.
10. Cook the chicken rolls in the skillet for 2-3 minutes on each side, until golden brown.
11. Transfer the chicken rolls to a baking dish and bake in the preheated oven for 15-20 minutes, or until the chicken is cooked through and the cheese is melted.
12. Serve the chicken cordon bleu hot, garnished with chopped parsley if desired.

Chateaubriand

Prep: 20 minutes – Cook: 50 minutes – Servings: 2
Calories: 340 – Fat 19 – Carbs: 3g – Fiber: 1g – Sugar: 1g – Protein 32g

Chateaubriand is a dish that is traditionally made with a tenderloin steak that is grilled or roasted and served with a red wine sauce.

Ingredients

- 2 (8-ounce) center-cut beef tenderloin steaks, about 1 ½" thick
- 1 cup dry red wine
- 2 tablespoons unsalted butter
- ½ cup finely chopped shallots
- 1 cup beef broth
- 2 tablespoons chopped fresh parsley
- 1 tablespoon olive oil
- Freshly ground black pepper & salt to taste

Directions

1. Preheat the oven to 400 F.
2. Rub the steaks with olive oil, then season them generously with salt and pepper.
3. Heat a large, oven-safe skillet over medium-high heat. Add the steaks to the skillet and cook until they are browned on both sides, about 2-3 minutes per side.
4. Transfer the skillet to the oven and roast the steaks for 10-12 minutes for medium-rare or until they reach your desired doneness.
5. Remove the skillet from the oven and transfer the steaks to a plate. Cover the steaks with foil and let them rest for 5 minutes.
6. Meanwhile, make the sauce. Heat the same skillet over medium heat. Add the butter and shallots and sauté until the shallots are softened, about 3-4 minutes.
7. Add the red wine and beef broth to the skillet and bring the mixture to a simmer. Cook until the liquid is reduced by half, stirring occasionally, about 10-12 minutes.
8. Stir in the parsley and season the sauce with salt and pepper to taste.
9. To serve, slice the steaks and arrange them on plates. Spoon the sauce over the top of the steaks and serve immediately.

Desserts

Pineapple Upside-Down Cake

Prep: 20 minutes – Cook: 35 minutes – Servings: 8
Calories: 400 – Fat 16g – Carbs: 54g – Fiber: 2g – Sugar: 34g – Protein 4g

Pineapple upside-down cake is a classic dessert that features a caramelized pineapple and brown sugar topping with a moist cake base.

Ingredients

For The Topping:
- ¼ cup unsalted butter
- 1 can (20 ounces) pineapple slices in juice, drained (reserve juice)
- ½ cup packed brown sugar
- Maraschino cherries

For The Cake:
- ½ cup pineapple juice (reserved from canned pineapple)
- 1 ½ cups all-purpose flour
- ¼ teaspoon baking soda
- 1 teaspoon baking powder
- ⅓ cup unsalted butter, softened
- 2 large eggs
- ¾ cup granulated sugar
- 1 teaspoon vanilla extract
- ¼ teaspoon salt

Directions

1. Preheat the oven to 350 F.
2. Melt the butter in a 9-inch cake pan in the oven.
3. Sprinkle brown sugar over the melted butter and arrange the pineapple slices on top of the sugar. Place a cherry in the center of each pineapple slice.
4. In a medium bowl, whisk together the flour, baking powder, baking soda, and salt.
5. In a separate large mixing bowl, beat the butter and sugar with an electric mixer until creamy and lightened in color.
6. Add the eggs one at a time, beating well after each addition.
7. Add the pineapple juice and vanilla extract and mix until well combined.
8. Gradually add the dry ingredients to the wet ingredients, mixing until just combined.
9. Pour the cake batter over the pineapple slices in the cake pan.
10. Bake for 35-40 minutes, or until a toothpick inserted in the center comes out clean.
11. Remove the cake from the oven and let it cool in the pan for 5 minutes.
12. Run a knife around the edges of the cake pan to loosen the cake, then invert the cake onto a serving platter, with the pineapple side up. Serve the cake warm or at room temperature.

Baked Alaska

Prep: 20 minutes – Cook: 25 minutes – Servings: 6
Calories: 444 – Fat 24g – Carbs: 54g – Fiber: 2g – Sugar: 40g – Protein 6g

Baked Alaska is a classic dessert that consists of ice cream and cake covered in meringue and baked in the oven until the meringue is lightly browned.

Ingredients

- 1 (9-inch) round cake, any flavor
- ¼ teaspoon cream of tartar
- 4 egg whites
- 1-quart vanilla ice cream, slightly softened
- ½ cup granulated sugar

Directions

1. Preheat the oven to 500 F.
2. Line a baking sheet with parchment paper and place the cake on top.
3. Cut the ice cream into 1-inch slices and arrange them on top of the cake, covering it completely. Smooth the top with a spatula.
4. Place the cake and ice cream in the freezer for at least 1 hour to firm up.
5. Meanwhile, make the meringue. In a large mixing bowl, beat the egg whites and cream of tartar with an electric mixer until frothy.
6. Gradually add the sugar to the egg whites, beating on high speed until stiff peaks form.
7. Remove the cake and ice cream from the freezer and spread the meringue over the top and sides, making sure to cover the ice cream completely.
8. Use a spatula to create peaks and swirls in the meringue.
9. Place the cake in the preheated oven and bake for 3-5 minutes, or until the meringue is lightly browned.
10. Remove the cake from the oven and serve immediately or return it to the freezer until ready to serve.

Chocolate Soufflé

Prep: 10 minutes – Cook: 35 minutes – Servings: 8
Calories: 394 – Fat 24g – Carbs: 40g – Fiber: 3g – Sugar: 24g – Protein 7g

Chocolate soufflé is a decadent dessert that is light and airy in texture

Ingredients

- ⅓ cup granulated sugar
- 2 tablespoons unsalted butter, softened
- 6 ounces bittersweet chocolate, chopped
- ½ cup whole milk
- 3 large eggs, separated
- Pinch of salt
- ⅛ teaspoon cream of tartar
- Powdered sugar, for garnish

Directions

1. Preheat the oven to 375 F. Butter four 6-ounce ramekins and sprinkle with sugar, tapping out any excess.
2. Melt the chocolate and butter in a double boiler or a heatproof bowl set over a saucepan of simmering water. Stir occasionally until smooth. Remove from heat and let cool slightly.
3. In a small saucepan, heat the milk until simmering.
4. In a mixing bowl, whisk together the egg yolks and sugar until thick and pale. Gradually whisk in the hot milk.
5. Add the melted chocolate mixture and stir until combined.
6. In a separate mixing bowl, beat the egg whites with salt and cream of tartar until stiff peaks form.
7. Gently fold one-third of the egg whites into the chocolate mixture until combined. Add the remaining egg whites and gently fold until no white streaks remain.
8. Divide the batter among the prepared ramekins, filling each about ¾ full.
9. Place the ramekins on a baking sheet and bake for 12-14 minutes, or until the soufflés are puffed and set around the edges but still slightly jiggly in the center.
10. Dust with powdered sugar and serve immediately..

Charlotte Russe

Prep: 20 minutes – Cook: 50 minutes – Servings: 10
Calories: 400 – Fat 24g – Carbs: 40g – Fiber: 1g – Sugar: 29g – Protein 6g

Charlotte Russe is a classic dessert that originated in France. It typically consists of a mold lined with ladyfingers or sponge cake, filled with a creamy custard or mousse, and chilled until set

Ingredients

- 12-14 ladyfingers or sponge cake slices
- ¼ cup cornstarch
- 4 large egg yolks
- 1 tablespoon unsalted butter
- ½ cup granulated sugar
- 1 teaspoon vanilla extract
- 2 cups whole milk
- 1 cup heavy cream
- ¼ teaspoon salt
- Fresh berries or fruit, for garnish

Directions

1. Line the bottom and sides of a 9-inch springform pan with ladyfingers or sponge cake slices, trimming them as needed to fit snugly.
2. In a medium saucepan, whisk together the sugar, cornstarch, and salt. Gradually whisk in the milk until smooth.
3. In a mixing bowl, whisk together the egg yolks. Gradually whisk in the milk mixture.
4. Cook the mixture over medium heat, whisking constantly, until it thickens and comes to a boil.
5. Remove from heat and whisk in butter and vanilla extract
6. Transfer the mixture to a mixing bowl and let cool to room temperature, stirring occasionally.
7. In a separate mixing bowl, beat the heavy cream until stiff peaks form.
8. Gently fold the whipped cream into the cooled custard mixture until well combined.
9. Pour the custard into prepared pan, smoothing the top with a spatula.
10. Chill in the refrigerator for at least 4 hours, or until set.
11. To serve, remove the sides of the pan and garnish with fresh berries or fruit.

Fruit Cocktail with Chantilly Cream

Prep: 10 minutes – Cook: 10 minutes – Servings: 4
Calories: 240 – Fat 16g – Carbs: 29g – Fiber: 2g – Sugar: 24g – Protein 2g

Fruit cocktail with Chantilly cream is a sweet and refreshing dessert that is perfect for warm weather.

Ingredients

- 1 can of fruit cocktail, drained (or 2 cups of fresh fruit)
- 1 cup heavy cream
- ¼ cup granulated sugar
- 1 teaspoon vanilla extract

Directions

1. In a mixing bowl, beat the heavy cream, sugar, and vanilla extract until stiff peaks form.
2. Gently fold in the fruit cocktail or fresh fruit until well combined.
3. Serve immediately, garnished with fresh mint leaves if desired.

Opera Cake

Prep: 20 minutes – Cook: 2 hours & 50 minutes – Servings: 8
Calories: 494 – Fat 34g – Carbs: 32g – Fiber: 2g – Sugar: 29g – Protein 6g

Opera cake is a French dessert made up of layers of almond sponge cake soaked in coffee syrup, chocolate ganache, and buttercream.

Ingredients

For the almond sponge cake:
- 4 eggs
- ½ cup granulated sugar
- 1 cup almond flour
- ½ cup all-purpose flour
- ¼ teaspoon salt

For the coffee syrup:
- ½ cup brewed coffee
- ¼ cup granulated sugar

For the chocolate ganache:
- 6 ounces dark chocolate, chopped
- ½ cup heavy cream

For the buttercream:
- 4 egg yolks
- ½ cup granulated sugar
- ¼ cup water
- 2 sticks unsalted butter, softened
- ½ teaspoon vanilla extract

Directions

1. Preheat the oven to 350 F. Line a baking sheet with parchment paper.
2. In a mixing bowl, beat the eggs and sugar on high speed until pale and fluffy.
3. In a separate bowl, mix together the almond flour, all-purpose flour, and salt.
4. Gently fold the dry ingredients into the egg mixture until well combined.
5. Pour the batter onto the prepared baking sheet and bake for 10-12 minutes, or until lightly golden and a toothpick comes out clean.
6. While the cake is baking, make the coffee syrup by mixing together the brewed coffee and sugar until the sugar dissolves.
7. Make the chocolate ganache by heating the heavy cream in a small saucepan until it begins to simmer. Pour the cream over the chopped chocolate and stir until the chocolate has melted and the mixture is smooth.
8. For the buttercream, beat the egg yolks until pale and fluffy. In a small saucepan, heat the sugar and water over medium-high heat until it reaches 238 F on a candy thermometer. Gradually pour the sugar syrup into the egg yolks while continuing to beat on high speed. Beat until the mixture has cooled to room temperature.
9. Add the softened butter and vanilla extract to the egg yolk mixture and beat on high speed until the buttercream is smooth and creamy.
10. Assemble the opera cake by cutting the almond sponge cake into 3 equal rectangles. Brush each layer with the coffee syrup, then spread a layer of chocolate ganache and buttercream on top of each layer. Top with the final layer of almond sponge cake.
11. Chill the cake in the fridge for at least 2 hours, or until the buttercream has set. Slice and serve.

Strawberry Shortcake

Prep: 20 minutes – Cook: 50 minutes – Servings: 8
Calories: 494 – Fat 34g – Carbs: 32g – Fiber: 2g – Sugar: 29g – Protein 6g

Strawberry shortcake is a classic dessert that consists of a sweet biscuit or sponge cake layered with fresh strawberries and whipped cream.

Ingredients

For the biscuits:
- 2 cups all-purpose flour
- ⅓ cup granulated sugar
- 2 teaspoons baking powder
- ½ teaspoon baking soda
- ½ teaspoon salt
- ½ cup unsalted butter, chilled and cubed
- ¾ cup buttermilk
- 1 large egg

For the strawberry filling:
- 1-pound fresh strawberries, hulled and sliced
- ¼ cup granulated sugar

For the whipped cream:
- 1 cup heavy cream
- ¼ cup powdered sugar
- ½ teaspoon vanilla extract

Directions

1. Preheat the oven to 400 F. Line a baking sheet with parchment paper.
2. In a large mixing bowl, whisk together the flour, sugar, baking powder, baking soda, and salt.
3. Add the chilled cubed butter to the flour mixture and use a pastry cutter or your fingers to work the butter into the flour until the mixture is crumbly.
4. In a separate bowl, whisk together the buttermilk and egg. Pour the buttermilk mixture into the flour mixture and stir until a sticky dough forms.
5. Turn the dough out onto a floured surface and knead gently until the dough comes together. Pat the dough into a 1-inch thickness and use a biscuit cutter to cut out biscuits. Place the biscuits onto the prepared baking sheet.
6. Bake the biscuits for 12-15 minutes, or until they are lightly golden on top. Remove from the oven and let cool.
7. While the biscuits are baking, prepare the strawberry filling by mixing together the sliced strawberries and sugar in a bowl. Let sit for 15-20 minutes to allow the sugar to dissolve and the strawberries to release their juices.
8. To make the whipped cream, whip the heavy cream, powdered sugar, and vanilla extract together in a mixing bowl until stiff peaks form.
9. To assemble the strawberry shortcakes, split each biscuit in half and spoon a generous amount of the strawberry filling on the bottom half. Top with a dollop of whipped cream and replace the top half of the biscuit. Serve immediately..

Raspberry Meringue

Prep: 20 minutes – Cook: 50 minutes – Servings: 4
Calories: 94 – Fat 0g – Carbs: 24g – Fiber: 1g – Sugar: 24g – Protein 2g

Raspberry Meringue is a light and airy dessert that is perfect for special occasions.

Ingredients

- 4 egg whites
- 1 cup granulated sugar
- ½ teaspoon cream of tartar
- 1 teaspoon vanilla extract
- ½ cup fresh raspberries
- Whipped cream (optional)

Directions

1. Preheat the oven to 300 F. Line a baking sheet with parchment paper.
2. In a mixing bowl, beat the egg whites and cream of tartar on high speed until stiff peaks form.
3. Gradually add in the sugar, one tablespoon at a time, while continuing to beat on high speed.
4. Add in the vanilla extract and beat for another 1-2 minutes.
5. Gently fold in the raspberries, being careful not to overmix.
6. Using a spoon or piping bag, form mounds of the meringue mixture on the prepared baking sheet.
7. Bake for 40-45 minutes or until the meringues are lightly golden and crisp on the outside.
8. Serve immediately, topped with whipped cream if desired.

Jellied Fruit Terrine

Prep: 20 minutes – Cook: 4 hours & 5 minutes – Servings: 8
Calories: 94 – Fat 1g – Carbs: 20g – Fiber: 2g – Sugar: 14g – Protein 2g

Jellied fruit terrine is a classic dessert that features layers of fruit suspended in a gelatin mixture

Ingredients

- 2 envelopes unflavored gelatin
- 2 cups boiling water
- ¼ cup granulated sugar
- 1 tablespoon fresh lemon juice
- ¼ teaspoon salt
- 2 cups mixed fresh fruit (such as strawberries, kiwi, grapes, and blueberries), diced
- Cooking spray

Directions

1. In a large bowl, whisk together the gelatin, boiling water, sugar, lemon juice, and salt until the gelatin is completely dissolved.
2. Let the mixture cool to room temperature.
3. While the gelatin mixture cools, prepare the fruit by washing, peeling, and dicing as necessary.
4. Lightly spray a 9-inch loaf pan with cooking spray.
5. Once the gelatin mixture has cooled, pour a thin layer of it into the bottom of the prepared pan.
6. Arrange a layer of fruit on top of the gelatin, making sure the fruit is evenly distributed.
7. Pour another layer of the gelatin mixture over the fruit, covering it completely.
8. Repeat with another layer of fruit and gelatin until all the fruit and gelatin mixture has been used.
9. Cover the pan with plastic wrap and refrigerate for at least 4 hours, or until the gelatin has set.
10. Once the gelatin has set, run a knife along the edges of the pan to loosen the terrine.
11. Invert the terrine onto a serving platter and slice into even portions.

Sign-up Now
and Be Notified of New Books

Website: readbooks.today

Printed in Great Britain
by Amazon